Every Life

IS BEAUTIFUL

The OCTOBER**BABY** Bible Study

written by **Nic Allen**

based on the film by **Jon** and **Andrew Erwin**

screenplay by **Theresa Preston** and **Jon Erwin**

LifeWay Press®
Nashville, TN

Published by LifeWay Press®
© 2012 Gravitas, LLC

ISBN: 978-1-4158-7397-7 • Item 005506648

Dewey Decimal classification: 248.843
Subject headings: CHRISTIAN LIFE \ WOMEN \ FORGIVENESS \ ABORTION

Scripture quotations are taken from the Holman Christian Standard Bible®, Copyright © 1999, 2000,
2002, 2003, 2009 by Holman Bible Publishers. Used by permission. Holman Christian Standard
Bible®, Holman CSB®, and HCSB® are federally registered trademarks of Holman Bible Publishers.

To order additional copies of this resource:
Write LifeWay Church Resources Customer Service; One LifeWay Plaza; Nashville, TN 37234-
0113; fax (615) 251-5933; phone (800) 458-2772; e-mail *orderentry@lifeway.com;* order online at
www.lifeway.com; or visit the LifeWay Christian Store serving you.

Printed in the United States of America

Leadership and Adult Publishing, LifeWay Christian Resources,
One LifeWay Plaza, Nashville, TN 37234-0175

Contents

About the Authors

THE ERWIN BROTHERS

OCTOBER BABY director team Jon and Andrew Erwin have been working in the entertainment industry for many years. Both began their careers as sports cameramen for ESPN.

In 2005 the pair ventured into directing commercials and music videos. They found their greatest success in the world of music, directing music videos and producing concerts and television programs for platinum artists and groups like Amy Grant, Michael W. Smith, Third Day, and Casting Crowns. The Erwin brothers have received 10 nominations and back-to-back wins for Music Video of The Year at the GMA Dove Awards.

Recently, the brothers completed a feature-length documentary titled *The Mysterious Islands* on location in the Galapagos.

Andy and Jon are based in Birmingham, Alabama, where they own their own production company. Filmed in various locations across Alabama, *OCTOBER BABY* is their first feature film.

NIC ALLEN worked alongside the Erwin brothers to develop this Bible study. He serves Rolling Hills Community Church in Franklin, Tennessee, as Family and Children's Pastor. Similarly, he worked with Sherwood Baptist Church to develop *Courageous Living Bible Study*. Nic and his wife have experience in crisis pregnancy counseling.

About the Movie

OCTOBER BABY is the coming-of-age story of Hannah, a beautiful 19-year-old college freshman. In spite of her energetic (if somewhat naïve) personality, Hannah has always felt like an outsider. Something is missing. She has always carried a deep-seated sense that she has no right to exist.

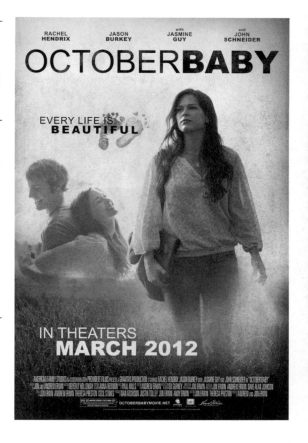

When she discovers she was adopted it comes as a shock, but Hannah's world is rocked even more when she learns why she was never told before—because she is the survivor of a failed abortion. Desperate for answers, she embarks on a road trip with some friends (including her oldest and closest friend, Jason) to find her biological mother.

Ultimately Hannah discovers that true freedom can be found in the words "I forgive you" as she discovers who she is and the peace to live the life she has always dreamed.

This uplifting and beautiful film may change the way you look at the world, your loved ones, and life itself. You can visit www.octoberbabymovie.net and www.lifeway.com/octoberbaby for updates and more information.

Every Life Is Beautiful

What is your definition of a nightmare? Is it the dream when you're falling but never hit the ground? The one in which you're being chased, seconds away from being caught just as you wake up in a cold sweat?

Perhaps your biggest nightmare doesn't just come out at night while you sleep. Maybe it's the fear of losing a child or your job or being unable to mend a broken marriage. What if your worst nightmare were not something you could imagine or predict but something that came out of nowhere and shook the foundation of your life?

That's the story of Hannah Lawson. In many respects, her life is to be envied—successful parents, great friends, a bright future. In other ways, she has faced challenges to which many of us could never relate—several surgeries, various health concerns, deep feelings of loneliness and despair.

In *OCTOBER BABY*, Hannah discovers the root of her physical and emotional problems: She is an abortion survivor. She woke up one morning with parents she loved and trusted only to discover that she was adopted but never told, almost aborted but surviving instead.

Hannah's nightmare is losing who she is. *OCTOBER BABY* is a journey in which she discovers that who she thought she was doesn't matter as much as who God made her to be. The movie is a powerful picture of a young woman who learns that life is beautiful, each and every part of it.

OCTOBER BABY is as much a film about the beauty of life as it is the sanctity of human life. Hannah may be looking for her biological mother but, along the way, she finds herself and a renewed faith in God. The characters are complex enough to relate to on many levels, even if the specific details of the story don't match any part of your story.

Think of this Bible study resource as an opportunity to jump into a swimming pool. The characters and clips are the diving board, but the Word of God is the water. Each session introduces you to an idea about your relationship with Christ through portions of the film that gives you a jumping-off point to consider your own story. Where you land when you take the leap is in the middle of a biblical text that will stretch you to evaluate how your life and your story align with the truth of God's Word.

Our prayer as you make this journey is that you will discover new truth about God and be challenged to openly live that truth. Life is beautiful. It's composed of stories that make it real, sometimes raw, but always rich with opportunity to live out the redemptive story of Jesus.

How to Use This Study

You are engaging in a Bible study about life, and every life has a story to share. Each week of *Every Life Is Beautiful: The OCTOBER BABY Bible Study* is organized into four sections and can be used for small-group or personal study.

Share, the introductory section for each week, includes icebreaker activities and questions to promote personal thinking and sharing. Engage in these opportunities to be more transparent and to get to know the members of your group.

Read the questions and be prepared to reflect, write, and share your thoughts as appropriate. Some questions may be more for private reflection than group sharing. No one is ever required to share.

Watch is the time your group views a video clip from *OCTOBER BABY* and discusses the questions that accompany it. The Bible study DVD contains clips for each of the four sessions; each clip is four to seven minutes long. You can visit *www.lifeway.com/octoberbaby* for downloads of these clips.

Study is the Bible study section, the primary focus of each session. Learners read a portion of Scripture and are prompted to discuss questions related to the Bible passage.

Live includes a lesson summary and reflection activities. A Challenge for the coming week can help participants begin to live with hope, forgiveness, and faith in the area of study.

In a variety of ways throughout *Every Life Is Beautiful: The OCTOBER BABY Bible Study,* learners are challenged to log and begin to share a part of their God story.

A Note to Leaders

Thank you for leading this study. While you will view the movie clips as a part of your session, learners should take time to engage the study on their own throughout the week. Encourage participants to spend time reading through the Scriptures and responding to prompts in the Share and Live sections so they are prepared to glean the most from the group experience. Ask them to come ready, having read the Scriptures and the Study section if possible.

This film will likely strike a nerve with people. Abortion is a polarizing issue, even within the church. Dr. David Platt delivered a solid word about abortion at the Secret Church event in November 2011, titled "Marriage, Family, Sex, and the Gospel." One teaching session centered on man's distortions of each. The truth of God's Word was spoken to shed light on divorce, homosexuality, pornography, polygamy, and abortion.[1] (Visit *www.lifeway.com/secretchurch* for future Secret Church events and information.)

The bottom line on any biblically-based discussion about abortion is that God alone is the judge of sin and each sinner; we are not. He alone is the Savior of sinners (all of us) and the Healer of the broken (all of us, at some time). Our responsibility as forgiven people is to point others to God and His grace—including those who have been impacted by abortion.

While abortion is certainly the underlying issue, it is not the central feature of *OCTOBER BABY* or this study. Encourage your group not to become divisive on political views surrounding abortion but to focus instead on the driving issues illumined by this study.

Every life is beautiful.
To be human is to be flawed. Secrets do have the power to destroy, but we have the choice to diffuse them.

Only in Jesus can we be fully alive.
An identity wrapped in anything else is idolatry.

Forgiveness is not easy—nor is it an option for the Christ follower.
Because we have been forgiven, we have the power to forgive.
Obedience to God's Word means that we must forgive.

Restoration means renewal.
It's about a new birth and a new day to better become the person God has called and equipped you to be.

This study can indeed provide a link to Christ's healing for the post-abortive woman. It can become an encouragement for the young adult struggling to identify with Christ fully. This small-group experience can be a reminder for all believers to be honest, Christ-centered, and forgiveness-driven in every area of life, regardless of the issue.

OCTOBER BABY and the *Every Life Is Beautiful* study can also be a point of serendipity for the abortion survivor. Perhaps this study will be that moment in time when you latch onto God's truth and find hope. Allow yourself to bask in His gracious love and purpose for you—to live a purposeful, ministering, beautiful life.

Leaders, as you facilitate this experience, might I encourage you to be vulnerable about your own life and struggles? Your group will take its authenticity cue from you. The members in your group will likely only go as deep and be as open as you are willing to be. Know that as this work is being prepared for print, you are being prayed for. May God bless you and those you minister to through this experience.

Guidelines for Small Groups

Confidentiality
As you dive into small-group Bible study, group members will be prompted to share thoughts, feelings, and personal experiences. Experiences may surface that have never been shared before, and healing and restoration can begin. Any and all expressions should be made out of trust and kept with strictest confidence by the group. At the same time, no one should be forced to share.

Respect
As trust forms and participants begin to open up about their personal experiences and even past mistakes, it might become easy to offer quick advice. Scripture teaches us to be quick to listen and slow to speak (see Jas. 1:19). Listening is the key to respect. Even well-meaning advice can be ill-received if it is not requested.

Commit to respect each others' opinions and to provide a safe place for them to be shared without fear of judgment or unsolicited advice.

Preparation
Get the most out of this Bible study by coming to group having read through the study and answered the questions, ready to discuss the material. Each participant can respect the contribution of others by taking time to prepare for each session.

Accountability
The goal of any small-group experience is transformation. Each week, participants will be asked to commit to share how God is moving in their lives. As individuals and as a group, commit to the accountability necessary to staying the course and living a beautiful life.

I commit to these principles for myself and my group
as I participate in Every Life Is Beautiful.

The Truth About Secrets

Every life has a story to share and every part of our life comprises our story. The secrets we keep can threaten the power of our story. In an effort to be transparent and to get to know your group, share a brief response to the following questions.

Name a favorite childhood memory.
Describe your high-school "self" in three words or less.
What is your favorite thing about life right now?
What is one way your group can pray for you through this experience?

Jeannie St. John Taylor is the author of numerous children's books, including *You Wouldn't Love Me If You Knew*. It's the story of a young boy who does something wrong and is afraid he can never be forgiven. He tries to replace his mistake with a series of good deeds but never feels "good enough" as a result. After coming clean, he learns a powerful truth about God's forgiveness.[1]

Do you recall ever feeling unforgiveable? What did you learn?

Taylor's book may be intended for 5- to 8-year-olds, but the concept is ageless. More than a few times you may have thought—even uttered—that people would not (*like, love, accept, befriend, trust,* or *forgive;* insert the correct word) you if they knew your deepest, most private self.

Privately reflect on your response to one of these questions.
If you are currently harboring a secret, why do you think you are afraid to be honest and open?

At a time you "came clean" about a secret, how did the important people in your life respond? How have those relationships suffered or benefited from your vulnerability?

VIEW CLIP 1 from the small-group DVD and discuss to start your study.

SUMMARY In this scene, Hannah Lawson locates and confronts her biological mom, only to be let down. Cindy Hastings has put the past behind her and built a life she loves. Successful career, marriage, and family indicate a woman who "has it all."

Cindy also has a painful secret she has worked hard to cover up, even to the extent of changing her name. Now face-to-face with Hannah, the evidence of her hidden past, Cindy has to decide whether to accept the truth or hold onto her lie.

OPEN DISCUSSION Cindy Hastings wanted to terminate her pregnancy. For 19 years, she lived with the truth that her failed attempt resulted in the birth of two children, one of whom died. The movie doesn't tell us how much she knew about Hannah's survival or health issues. We cannot be certain what Cindy knew about Hannah's adoption or her life. We can be sure she was very surprised by the encounter.

1 How did you feel after seeing this scene in the theater and in the movie clip today?

Hannah was dealing with a lot of emotion about the cover-ups in her life. Her adoptive parents had concealed the truth about her birth and her brother for her entire childhood. Now having located her biological mom, she was looking for answers her adoptive parents had not given her.

2 How do you think Hannah felt when Cindy denied her the truth she was seeking? In what ways do you relate to Hannah in this scene?

Sometimes people think they are protecting themselves or even another person when they hide truth. Covering up shame with a lie may seem like the easiest choice. Unfortunately, it leads to more of the same—secrecy, concealing the past, lies, and shame.

3 Has someone close to you ever concealed the truth from you? How did that make you feel? How did you respond when you learned the truth?

4 In what ways can you relate to Cindy's response in this scene?

study

Aren't you glad that the life of David is chronicled in Scripture? Aren't you encouraged that even the lineage of Jesus is riddled with flawed characters? We certainly see ourselves in them!

David is described as loyal, a man after God's own heart (see 1 Sam. 13:14), and this truth is evidenced many moments in his story. We also know that David was a man with great sin. His affair with Bathsheba and murder of her husband Uriah are unthinkable.

To familiarize yourself with the story, read Nathan's summary of David's sin in 2 Samuel 12:1-12.

How is it easier to see sin in someone else than to see it in ourselves? (See v. 5.)

What does Nathan say will be the result of David's sin?

Read 1 Samuel 12:13-15.

How does David respond when his sin is uncovered?

David saw the sin in the rich man before recognizing the sin in his own life. In response to Nathan's admonition, David did admit his guilt in verse 13. Nathan assured David that he was forgiven and would not die as a result of this sin but the additional consequences of his actions would remain. The son David fathered with Bathsheba would die. Although David fasted and pleaded with God (see 2 Sam. 12:16-17), the baby died.

How are you impacted by knowing that David was forgiven but still had to endure the consequence of his sin?

Read Psalm 32.

¹How joyful is the one
whose transgression is forgiven,
whose sin is covered!
²How joyful is the man
the Lᴏʀᴅ does not charge with sin
and in whose spirit is no deceit!
³When I kept silent, my bones became brittle
from my groaning all day long.
⁴For day and night Your hand was heavy on me;
my strength was drained
as in the summer's heat.
⁵Then I acknowledged my sin to You
and did not conceal my iniquity.
I said, "I will confess my transgressions to the Lᴏʀᴅ,"
and You took away the guilt of my sin.
⁶Therefore let everyone who is faithful pray to You
at a time that You may be found.
When great floodwaters come,
they will not reach him.
⁷You are my hiding place;
You protect me from trouble.
You surround me with joyful shouts of deliverance.
⁸I will instruct you and show you the way to go;
with My eye on you, I will give counsel.
⁹Do not be like a horse or mule,
without understanding,
that must be controlled with bit and bridle
or else it will not come near you.
¹⁰Many pains come to the wicked,
but the one who trusts in the Lᴏʀᴅ
will have faithful love surrounding him.
¹¹Be glad in the Lᴏʀᴅ and rejoice,
you righteous ones;
shout for joy, all you upright in heart.

Psalm 32 is classified as one of seven penitential songs of the early church.[2] David wrote this poem as a confession of his sin but also as a litany of lessons learned. Verse 3 indicates David's secret. "When I kept silent," he begins. While we cannot hide our sin from God, the very attempt to keep our sin secret weighs on us.

> According to verses 3-4, how did David's sin and guilt make him feel physically and emotionally? What are some ways you see sin and guilt affecting people you know?

> According to verse 5, what specifically did David do and what specifically did God do?

DAVID	GOD

The Holman Christian Standard Bible uses the words "acknowledged" and "confess" in verse 5. Both come from the same Hebrew root which means "to know."[3] The concept of confession in Hebrew also means the physical act of casting or throwing down. When we acknowledge our sin before God and confess our sin to Him, we are claiming that we *know* what we did was wrong and offensive to holy God. And we are throwing it down before Him because He alone can carry that load and forgive our sin.

Now read verses 6-11.

> Identify lessons David learned about sin and secrets.

David sinned when he took Bathsheba. When she became pregnant, he sinned again by trying to manipulate the situation so the baby appeared to be Uriah's. He sinned further when he had Uriah killed. David's adultery dishonored God, and his desire to keep that act a secret magnified his sin.

It would be easy to evaluate David's sins as more grave than our own. The consequences were certainly severe. A man lost his life. A woman lost her husband. David and Bathsheba lost a child. Without judging David too harshly, consider the sin(s) you have committed and attempted to cover.

> How have you been (or how are you living now) like David the sinner?

Read Psalm 51:1-5 for a deeper look at David's confession.

¹Be gracious to me, God,
according to Your faithful love;
according to Your abundant compassion,
blot out my rebellion.
²Wash away my guilt
and cleanse me from my sin.
³For I am conscious of my rebellion,
and my sin is always before me.
⁴Against You—You alone—I have sinned
and done this evil in Your sight.
So You are right when You pass sentence;
You are blameless when You judge.
⁵Indeed, I was guilty when I was born;
I was sinful when my mother conceived me.

> How have you been (or how are you living now) like David the forgiven?

Shakespeare's *Macbeth* is a telling tale of sin and secrets. It's also a story of how guilt and shame overwhelm us. Lord and Lady Macbeth committed many an extra sin to conceal and cover up the first one. In a significant line, Macbeth tells Lady Macbeth, "False face must hide what the false heart doth know" (act 1, scene 7).[4] In other words, we've done horrible things and now we must put on a false self to hide the truth about ourselves.

People's perception of you is based on what you allow them to know about you. It's out of fear and guilt that we do not allow people to see our true selves. We put on airs and go so far as to tell outright lies in order to control the image we portray about who we really are.

Understand these truths about secrets:
1. Secrets birth other secrets.
2. Secrets make us lonely.
3. Secrets disconnect us from others.
4. Secrets are not secrets from God, but they do strain our relationship with Him.
5. Secrets prevent us from being fully alive in Christ.
6. Secrets lose their power when they are shared.

It is when we confess our sin to God that He forgives us and removes our fear and guilt. It is when we walk in the freedom of that forgiveness that we don't have to hide any more. It is when, like David, we come clean with God that we enjoy favor with Him again.

YOUR CHALLENGE NEXT WEEK

During the coming week take an opportunity to journal your response to one of the questions on this page; you choose. Then be challenged to open up and share this part of your story with a trusted person this week. It can be your spouse, another family member, or close friend. Share that your Bible study is challenging you to be more transparent and ask whether he or she would allow you to share what you are learning, including part of your personal story.

Perhaps you are doing this study with a group. If so, your leader may carve out time each week for those who would like to share their journal entries to do so.

Choose to answer one of these questions.

1   What is something about your *personality* that not many people know? Write about and share it with someone this week.

2   What is something you have *overcome* that not many people know? Write about and share it with someone this week.

3   What is something with which you *struggle* that not many people know? Write about and share it with someone you trust this week. If needed, follow up with your pastor, mentor, trusted friend, or accountability partner about seeking further help with this issue.

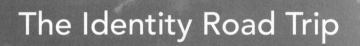

The Identity Road Trip

Think about the last time you saw a newborn. How long did it take before family resemblance made its way into the conversation? "He's got his mom's eyes." "Look at those dimples!" "Those curls are like his brother's."

From the time a baby enters the world, connections to where she came from enter the scene. Conclusions are drawn as to who a child will grow to be like based on traits indicated by behaviors. As a child develops, physical characteristics aren't the only traits we notice. Personalities, habits, and mannerisms are born and raised in the context of family.

Who do people say that you look like? act like?

If you are a parent (or hope to be some day), which of your character traits do you hope your children possess? Which ones do you hope pass them by?

Take a few moments to respond to one of the following questions.
Describe the family in which you grew up. What made your family unique?

If you are adopted, how do you feel when you hear others talk about babies and which parent they look like?

When did you realize who you were? What circumstances and people influenced your understanding of identity?

VIEW CLIP 2 from the small-group DVD and discuss to start your study.

SUMMARY In this scene, Hannah is on a dock, a place she comes to often and a place where Jason can easily find her. In one of those "I don't want to talk about it" moments, we discover that she desperately does want to talk. She has so many unanswered questions, but they all boil down to one that she most desires to know: Who is she? Hannah feels stuck and wants to move on, but, in a moment of identity crisis, she has no idea how or where to start.

OPEN DISCUSSION Research names adolescence as the life stage in which identity becomes paramount.[1] It's no wonder that 19-year-old Hannah set out on a quest to find herself. While her story is completely unique, Hannah's desire to figure out who she is and to define for herself an identity is quite a normal part of adolescent development.

1 As you were growing up, in what ways did you define yourself or attempt to find yourself?

2 How does that differ with how you define yourself today? List all the identity markers you can think of, such as important relationships, as well as the roles you wear personally and professionally.

Women tend to define themselves within the context of relationships.[2] "I am Katie's mom and Doug's wife." "I'm a loving mom, caring sister, and genuine friend. "For most men, social development involves a move toward autonomy in relationships in order to strengthen identity and create individuality. They tend to define themselves in terms of roles and accomplishments.[3] Examples might be, "I am an accountant." "I was named top salesman for my district for the third year."

An identity crisis is defined as "a psychosocial state or condition of disorientation and role confusion occurring especially in adolescents as a result of conflicting internal and external experiences, pressures, and expectations and often producing acute anxiety."[4] Hannah lived 19 years under one set of suppositions. It's easy to understand why she would feel confused and anxious.

Perhaps you have been in a situation when you have lost some part of your identity. You were laid off from a job or endured a divorce. You had to face the tragic loss of someone you loved. You faced a significant health scare or cross-country move. People go to great lengths to protect their identity.

Challenges to our identity come from all directions. The item you consider most significant on your identity-markers list is probably the area in which you would experience the greatest challenge. If you have not yet faced such a crisis of identity, consider for just a moment how you might respond.

3 What is your definition or understanding of identity in Christ?

If it weren't for Paul, we would be missing half of the New Testament. Much of our doctrine would be full of holes. Outside of Christ, he is the Bible character who has had the most influence on our New Covenant faith.

But Paul (formerly called "Saul") didn't start out that way. The story of Paul's conversion is powerful because of what he converted from as well as Whom he converted to. Paul claimed to be the chief of sinners (see 1 Tim. 1:15) while we would herald him the chief of Christians.

Familiarize yourself with Paul's history and conversion by reading Acts 8:1-3; 9:1-31.

A broad overview of his New Testament writings gives us an inside scoop on the identity of this most-published apostle.

Read the following passages of Scripture and outline the ways that Paul characterized himself.

Philippians 3:3-6   Acts 22:2-5,28-29   Galatians 2:18-20

Paul had every reason to rest on his worldly identity. By Jewish standards, he was without compare. By Roman standards, he was a citizen with good standing. But in God's economy, none of that mattered compared to being filled with Christ.

Read Philippians 3:7-10.

> [7]Everything that was a gain to me, I have
> considered to be a loss because of Christ.
> [8]More than that, I also consider everything to be a loss
> in view of the surpassing value of knowing Christ Jesus
> my Lord. Because of Him I have suffered the loss of all
> things and consider them filth, so that I may gain Christ
> [9]and be found in Him, not having a righteousness of my
> own from the law, but one that is through faith in Christ—
> the righteousness from God based on faith.
> [10]My goal is to know Him and the power of His resurrection and
> the fellowship of His sufferings, being conformed to His death.

Paul considered everything a loss when compared to knowing Jesus Christ. That means that Paul viewed every status, privilege, and title as nothing but loss when it came to Jesus. Everything that his heritage would have listed as profit was actually worthless in light of the glory of Christ Jesus.

In examining your list of identity markers on page 25, which one do you hold most dear?

What does it mean for you to consider that which you hold most precious to be a total loss when it comes to knowing Christ?

How does that play out practically in how you live?

The truth is, nothing which we cling to in this world has any certainty except Christ. An identity wrapped up in anything but Him is sad at best and has the potential to collapse right in front of us at worst. An identity built in Christ and Christ alone is the only totally fulfilling way to live.

Look up and read Jeremiah 2:4-13 in your Bible.

In this passage, to whom is God speaking through the prophet Jeremiah?

In contrast to all the nations Israel knew personally the one true and living God. His chosen people had forsaken Him for inanimate objects of wood and stone. Not only had they forsaken Him, they had attempted to replace Him in their lives.

Putting your faith in anything other than God is idolatry. Too often, we confuse idol worship with a false religion when, in reality, it can manifest itself as a false sense of security. If your sense of self and belonging come from a career, then that is idolatry. A career cannot fill the hole in anyone's life; only a faith-based relationship with Jesus can.

If your sense of self and identity come from any relationship other than with Jesus, then that is idolatry. Even a marriage cannot satisfy the longing of your soul the way Christ can.

"Broken cisterns symbolize pagan gods that could not give or sustain life."[5] Without Jesus, even the most God-honoring job is a broken cistern. Without Jesus, even the most solid marriage is just a broken cistern. They cannot hold water.

Which item on your identity-markers list do you struggle with most when it comes to finding your total self in Christ?

In other words, in the analogy Jeremiah used, which ones may have become broken cisterns for you?

live

Examine these Scriptures and the identifying truths they speak about believers in Jesus. Read the statements and verses aloud. The Bible contains dozens of others. The following are just a few to consider today.

1 **I am God's child.**
John 1:12: "To all who did receive Him, He gave them the right to be children of God, to those who believe in His name."

2 **I have been justified.**
Romans 5:1: "Since we have been declared righteous by faith, we have peace with God through our Lord Jesus Christ."

3 **I am Christ's friend.**
John 15:15: "I have called you friends, because I have made known to you everything I have heard from My Father."

4 **I belong to God.**
1 Corinthians 6:20: "You were bought at a price. Therefore glorify God in your body."

5 **I am a member of Christ's body.**
1 Corinthians 12:27: "You are the body of Christ, and individual members of it."

6 **I am assured all things work together for good of those who love God.**
Romans 8:28: "We know that all things work together for the good of those who love God: those who are called according to His purpose."

7 **I have redemption.**
Ephesians 1:7-8: "We have redemption in Him through His blood, the forgiveness of our trespasses, according to the riches of His grace that He lavished on us with all wisdom and understanding."

8 I have purpose.

Ephesians 2:10: "We are His creation, created in Christ Jesus for good works, which God prepared ahead of time so that we should walk in them."

9 I have access to the Father.

Ephesians 2:18: "Through Him we both have access by one Spirit to the Father."

10 I possess the mind of Christ.

1 Corinthians 2:16: "For who has known the Lord's mind, that he may instruct Him? But we have the mind of Christ."

11 I am victorious.

1 John 5:4: "Whatever has been born of God conquers the world. This is the victory that has conquered the world: our faith."

12 I am blameless.

1 Corinthians 1:8: "He will also strengthen you to the end, so that you will be blameless in the day of our Lord Jesus Christ."

13 I am set free.

Romans 8:2: "The Spirit's law of life in Christ Jesus has set you free from the law of sin and of death."[6]

(Additional "identity" passages related to post-abortion healing may be found in *Surrendering the Secret* [005123170], p. 99).

YOUR CHALLENGE NEXT WEEK

In the coming week take an opportunity to journal your response to at least one Challenge question. Then take the risk to open up and share this part of your story with someone. It can be your spouse, another family member, or a trusted friend. Share that your Bible study is encouraging you to be more transparent. Ask whether you could share what you are learning and part of your story.

Perhaps you are doing this study with a group. If so, your leader may carve out time each week for those who would like to share their journal entries to do so.

Choose to interact with one or more of these questions this week.

1   Which of the claims from the Scripture list is most comforting for you? Why?

2   Which of the claims from the Scripture list is most difficult for you to walk in daily? Why?

3   What part of your identity would you like to surrender and replace with an identity found solely in Christ? Remember, this doesn't mean that you walk away from this role or relationship. It means that you surrender it to Christ and, like Paul, consider it to be less than the supreme joy found in knowing Jesus.

The Power of Forgiveness

"To err is Humane; to Forgive, Divine."
—Alexander Pope, 1711[1]

It is not uncommon for a quote to outlive the author or its original context. People can quote movies they have never seen, books they have never read, and even people they will never know. This line is from Alexander Pope's "Essay on Criticism" about a literary shift in poetry. In modern use, the quote is probably rarely used to evaluate or criticize popular literature.

In many people's minds, this quote is probably given the status of Scripture, although it isn't found in the Bible and actually goes against the summary of New Testament teaching. While to err is certainly human, forgiveness shouldn't be left exclusively to the divine. It should be the most normal, natural thing for those who know and follow Christ to forgive.

> What is the world's opinion about forgiveness? How do worldly perceptions differ from what Scripture teaches about how Christ followers should live?

> What do you find most difficult—to seek forgiveness, receive forgiveness, or offer forgiveness? Why?

Take a few moments to respond to one of these journaling activities.
Describe the last time you needed forgiveness.

Describe the last time someone needed your forgiveness.

VIEW CLIP 3 from the small-group DVD and discuss to start your study.

SUMMARY Hannah finds herself in a church, alone and confused. She encounters a priest and pours out her situation. Hannah hates herself because of what she has discovered and for what she feels. She blames her birth mom for not wanting her, her adoptive parents for lying to her, and herself for not being able to let go and move forward.

OPEN DISCUSSION Imagine for a moment that you are Hannah and in the same situation. Your birth mom chose to abort you and, in the process, you lost a brother you didn't know you had. Your adoptive parents have kept this truth from you. In both cases, you confront but still don't get the answers or response that you desire or feel like you deserve.

1   Would forgiveness be an automatic response, a delayed reaction, or
    a withheld virtue for you in a similar situation? Why?

2   Do you feel like you have the power to *choose* to forgive?
    Why or why not?

The priest explains to Hannah that hatred is a burden she no longer needs
to carry and that true freedom can only be found in forgiveness.

3   In what ways can you relate to Hannah in this part of the scene?
    How have you found forgiveness to be difficult to offer or receive?

4   Based on the hurts in your life and the situations you have faced
    that required forgiveness, do the priest's words feel comforting
    or challenging to you? Why?

Read Matthew 18:21-35 in your own Bible.

In response to Peter's question about the quantity of forgiveness, Jesus offers to us what seems like a simple math equation: 70 x 7 = 490. A lazy interpretation might be to keep a list of the number of times we're wronged, withholding forgiveness and keeping a grudge when the 491st infraction is reached. Jesus told His followers that there really should be no end to our forgiveness. In typical Jesus fashion, He accompanied His truth with a parable, a teaching that His followers could understand.

What is significant about the forgiveness that the king offered compared to the forgiveness that the slave withheld?

Do you feel the weight of the sin from which you have been forgiven?

When we withhold forgiveness from someone else, we lessen the degree to which we understand Christ's forgiveness. When we look at forgiveness as an option, we speak to our own ignorance of the truly gracious blessing we have received from God.

Now read Luke 6:37-38.

What do these verses tell us about God's forgiveness?

Simply forgiving those who wrong us in no way qualifies us for forgiveness. Salvation is the free gift of God and we cannot earn His favor by works. A full and complete understanding of salvation means that nothing we do can satisfy the demand of sin in our life. Only faith in God can save us.

Knowing that, this reference in Luke 6 doesn't mean that forgiving others is a prerequisite to our receiving forgiveness from God. It is, however, one of the many indicators of our understanding and obedience to His lordship in our lives. If we refuse to forgive others, this might mean we haven't been reconciled to Him in the first place or it could reveal that we are not living in the fullness of our relationship with Him as a growing disciple.

Take a moment to examine your heart.

Have you settled your personal faith relationship with God?

Is there bitterness in your life toward someone else (or even yourself) that is keeping you from enjoying the fullness of the forgiveness you have received from God?

Read Colossians 3:12-13.

¹²God's chosen ones, holy and loved, put on heartfelt compassion, kindness, humility, gentleness, and patience, ¹³accepting one another and forgiving one another if anyone has a complaint against another. Just as the Lord has forgiven you, so you must also forgive.

Paul's letter to the Colossian church was a letter of warning against heresy and false teaching that had become a threat to the believers there. In chapter 2 Paul provides the list of things they are to abandon as false teaching, and in chapter 3 he gives the list of how they are to conduct themselves in light of their relationship with Christ. Within that list is a verse about forgiveness, the foundation of our faith.

In addition to living lives of compassion, kindness, humility, gentleness, and patience, we are to adopt an attitude of forgiveness. Paul explains: because we have been forgiven, we should also forgive others. Maybe we are never more like God than when we do offer forgiveness. Maybe Alexander Pope was right; the act of forgiveness is divine indeed.

Take a moment to pray and ask God to help you live a new life in Christ to the fullest; one that incorporates compassion, kindness, humility, gentleness, patience, and ultimately forgiveness.

Understanding that we have really been forgiven by God is difficult. Sometimes our own lack of faith in His generous grace is the issue and sometimes the Evil One piles on so much guilt over our sin, we cannot possibly comprehend a God who could love us out of that deep pit.

Take a moment to read the section that best reflects where you are in your life.

TO POST-ABORTIVE WOMEN OR COUPLES Maybe you relate to this movie more than the average viewer because, at one point in your life, you terminated a pregnancy. Please know that God dearly loves you. That act in your past is not outside the bounds of His loving mercy and gracious forgiveness. Our God desires to redeem your past for His good pleasure.

Imagine that the note Hannah wrote to Cindy was meant for you. Imagine that God Himself penned it. You are forgiven. You are not defined by that moment or any other moment of sin in your life.

If you have not already found a healing community where you can share the emotions that accompany abortion, take the step to find a post-abortive counseling group in your area. This burden is one you are not intended to carry at all, much less alone. This is also a piece of your story that God intends to use for His glory. It is a testimony that can be shared to point others toward Christ.

You are forgiven. You are loved. This part of you can be used greatly by our God.

TO ADOPTIVE PARENTS Maybe it was the sting of infertility that prompted you to adopt. Maybe it was the call of God to reach out and include a child in your family who had no parents. Whatever the reason, you chose to adopt. Thank you for that.

Start to finish, Scripture highlights God's heart for the orphan and the oppressed (see Ps. 68:5-6; Isa. 1:17; Matt. 18:5; Jas. 1:27). You likely sacrificed and spent a great deal of time and money to bring an adoptive child into your family. If there have been moments in your story where you did not feel like a "real" parent, please extinguish those in your mind. If there have been people who have made you feel less of a parent because of adoption, forgive them and commit to pray for them. You are a mom or dad regardless of biology.

The desire your son or daughter has or might one day have to understand their biological heritage is a natural one. Rather than feel threatened by their desire, be part of the process. Help them on their journey of self-discovery and of emotional healing. For your adopted child, this could be part of their transition into adulthood. When you became a parent, that is what you signed up for.

As followers of Christ, we have *all* been adopted into God's family (see Rom. 8:14-16). Use your story of adoption to help point your child and others to our adoption in Christ. This part of your testimony magnifies the glory of God.

TO ANYONE WHO HAS BEEN HURT BY THEIR PARENTS Maybe you relate to this movie because, like Hannah, you have been hurt by your parents, be they adoptive or biological. Please know that whatever hurt you encountered is likely not your fault. Whether it was as simple as a lie they told or as serious as abuse or neglect, God can heal your physical wounds and also your broken heart.

Be warned that whatever challenges you faced as a result of your upbringing can manifest in your life as well. It takes intentionality to *not* repeat the mistakes our moms and dads made. That intentionality starts with recognizing the ways we have been hurt, forgiving them for hurting us, and doing the hard work of not allowing that part of our pain to relive itself in our own behavior.

Know that God can use this part of your story to gain glory and point people to Him and to healing. Know that by forgiving your parents, you will experience freedom. Know that by forgiving them and walking free, you set a powerful example for others.

TO THOSE OF US WHO ARE SINNERS This section could be titled "To everyone." Romans 3:23 is clear: we are all sinners. Because of our sin, we deserve eternal separation from God. Regardless of the earthly magnitude of our sin (ranging from white lies to murder), we all deserve death. Just being born a sinful person earns us a place alongside the worst of this world's criminals.

We are wicked people, sinful from birth (see Ps. 51:5). The Evil One would have you walk in fear over the guilt of your sin. He would have you bound by the threat of losing your salvation from a God who he tells you could not possibly love a sinner like you.

Know that, contrary to Satan's whispers, God's love for you is boundless. It has the power to save you and the power to set you free (see Rom. 5:8; 6:23). Know that the gravity of your sin only serves to illuminate the glory of God's grace. You didn't earn it; you cannot lose it. God is so good.

Walk confidently in the forgiveness you have asked for and received and always be willing and ready to extend that to others for the things they do to wrong you. Because God has forgiven you, you have the power to forgive others. Walk freely in that power and rest in the confidence that Christ's sacrifice covers your sin. You are forgiven.

YOUR CHALLENGE NEXT WEEK

In the coming week, in the journaling space provided, take some time to respond to one or more of the situations you just read about on pages 39–41, as they apply to you. Then be challenged to open up and share this part of your story with someone this week. It can be your spouse, another family member, or trusted friend. Share that your Bible study is challenging you to better understand the magnitude of God's forgiveness. Ask whether you could share what you are learning and part of your story.

Perhaps you are doing this study with a group. If so, your leader may carve out time each week for those who would like to share their journal entries to do so.

Also look at some follow-up opportunities in case you are interested and want to know more about a specific topics. See pages 53 and 61 specifically.

If you have not yet settled your relationship with God (described in "Those of us who are sinners" on p. 41 and "Your Doorway to New Life" on p. 57), then talk with your group facilitator, a pastor, or other Christian friend who can help you take this first step toward healing forgiveness.

The Joy of Restoration

During week 1, you uncovered some truths about secrets. Becoming someone who is honest about your personal struggles automatically makes you someone with whom other people can be honest. In week 2, you discovered the life and identity that can only be found in Christ. When you are alive in Christ, others are drawn to you and the freedom you have found. Last week you examined the art of forgiveness. We are best able to do the hard work of forgiving others when we comprehend the greatness of God's forgiveness.

This week, we tackle restoration. Restoration is the powerful by-product of an authentic life lived fully in Christ and having experienced the forgiveness only He can offer.

Define *reconciliation* and *restoration* in your own words.

While these words differ in meaning and use throughout Scripture, we often use them interchangeably. We understand being made right with God as involving both restoration and reconciliation. We understand the change that happens in our lives because of Christ to reflect both. Something divine happens as a result of faith in our relationship with God and His forgiveness.

Take a moment to respond to one of the following activities.
Describe how you came to know Christ. What was your life like before you trusted Jesus for salvation? How did your salvation story unfold? What is your life like now that you are a Christian?

Put into words the feelings you have about forgiveness and the newness you feel because of Christ in your life.

VIEW CLIP 4 from the small-group DVD and discuss to start your study.

SUMMARY This scene is a montage of hope. The characters we have encountered throughout the film are resolved. Each character experiences growth and change, healing and restoration.

Cindy shares her secret past with her husband and experiences subsequent comfort. Mary goes back to work as a nurse, this time caring for newborns. The scene closes with Hannah heading off to school again, and we witness an ultimate expression of love given and love received. Hannah knows who she is and that she is loved.

OPEN DISCUSSION Each character in the film experiences transformation. There is a change in his or her relationship to God and to each other.

Note how each character experienced forgiveness and restoration.

1   With which character(s) do you most closely identify? Why?

2   In what ways have you seen this type of restoration in your life
    or in the life of someone you know well?

3   Reflect on what Hannah learned from the priest and on what you
    learned about forgiveness last week. How is forgiveness a necessary
    step toward restoration?

4   In what area of your life do you need to experience restoration
    or "new birth"?

Earlier you defined reconciliation and restoration in your own words. Now let's look at some standard theological definitions of each word.

> *Reconciliation*—this theological term comes from a Greek word that means to change or exchange. It literally bears the connotation of changing in one's relationship to God; going from being God's enemy to God's friend.[1]

> *Restoration*—this theological term is used throughout the Old and New Testaments in several figurative ways and is often synonymous with the word *renew.* In our context, restore is best described by David's use in Psalm 51. To restore is to make right following a sin against God. In the New Testament, eschatological views point to the prescribed new birth of the believer as restoration.[2]

In the New Testament, Peter may best exemplify what it means to be restored. We know him to be Christ's most outspoken disciple. We know his successes and his failures. He walked on water (see Matt. 14:22-33). He was named "Rock" by Jesus (see Matt. 16:18) but, in the same chapter, is called "Satan" (Matt. 16:23). Peter also denied Christ (see Mark 14:66-72).

Read the story of Peter's restoration in John 21:15-19.

[15]When they had eaten breakfast, Jesus asked Simon Peter,
"Simon, son of John, do you love Me more than these?"
"Yes, Lord," he said to Him, "You know that I love You."
"Feed My lambs," He told him.
[16]A second time He asked him, "Simon, son of John, do you love Me?"
"Yes, Lord," he said to Him, "You know that I love You."
"Shepherd My sheep," He told him.
[17]He asked him the third time, "Simon, son of John, do you love Me?"
Peter was grieved that He asked him the third time, "Do you love Me?"
He said, "Lord, You know everything! You know that I love You."
"Feed My sheep," Jesus said.

¹⁸"I assure you: When you were young, you would tie your belt
and walk wherever you wanted. But when you grow old, you will
stretch out your hands and someone else will tie you
and carry you where you don't want to go."
¹⁹He said this to signify by what kind of death he would glorify God.
After saying this, He told him, "Follow Me!"

The subtle difference in the words translated "love" in this passage is
enough to help us glean a better understanding of this exchange. Jesus
asks Peter twice if he loves him with the kind of love that indicates total
and unconditional commitment (vv. 15-16, *agapao*).

Peter is only able to respond by offering Jesus a friendly affection, a
brotherly love (*phileo*). Jesus is persistent, questioning whether Peter
could even muster that level of love for his Master.[3]

Peter's grief-filled final response affirmed Jesus' lordship (v. 17). He claimed
that Jesus should know; He is all-knowing, after all. The ultimate answer
to Jesus' question wouldn't come from Peter's response but from God's
knowledge of Peter's heart.[4]

Each time Jesus asks Peter about his love, He instructs him to do the work
of a shepherd: to feed, shepherd, and then feed His sheep.

What did Jesus mean by those instructions?

Let's backtrack to John 21:1-4.
¹After this, Jesus revealed Himself again to His disciples
by the Sea of Tiberias. He revealed Himself in this way:
²Simon Peter, Thomas (called "Twin"), Nathanael from Cana of Galilee,
Zebedee's sons, and two others of His disciples were together.

^{3}"I'm going fishing," Simon Peter said to them.
"We're coming with you," they told him. They went out and
got into the boat, but that night they caught nothing.
^{4}When daybreak came, Jesus stood on the shore.
However, the disciples did not know it was Jesus.

Where does Jesus first encounter His disciples in this post-resurrection appearance? What are they doing?

Peter had gone back to where he started, back on a fishing boat doing what he was doing when Jesus found and called him. One possible interpretation of verse 15, when Jesus asked Peter if he loved him "more than these," is that Jesus may have been referring to the fish. Did Peter love Jesus more than he loved his former life?[5]

Now read Jesus' concluding words to Peter in John 21:22.
"If I want him to remain until I come," Jesus answered,
"what is that to you? As for you, follow Me."

In spite of Peter's courtyard denial and his lackluster proclamation of love in this seaside conversation, Jesus invites Peter to come and follow Him. Remember that when God restores us, it's a spiritual renewal, a rebirth, and a fresh start after sin against Him. In spite of his sin and less-than-ideal expression of faith, Jesus still had it in mind to use Peter.

Read Acts 2:36.
"Let all the house of Israel know with certainty that God has
made this Jesus, whom you crucified, both Lord and Messiah!"

Pentecost Peter is a far cry from the courtyard Peter in Mark 14 who denied knowing Christ.

> How do you perceive Peter in Acts 2:36? Does he appear to be affectionate (*phileo*) toward Jesus or passionately committed to Him *(agapao)*?

There could be no question that day about Peter's allegiance and faith. The beauty of Christ's forgiveness comes in the restoration. We are given new life and new purpose.

> How have you experienced God using you in light of being forgiven and restored?

> How can God's usefulness be magnified in your life as you seek to forgive and restore your earthly relationships?

In the restoration process, it's one thing for Christ to do the work of renewal in our lives and begin to use us for His good pleasure. It's an altogether different type of restoration when it comes to our human relationships. Christ did the work of reconciliation and restoration on the cross. There can be no more painstaking, difficult road toward restoration. As a result, restoration in our relationships will take sacrifice.

Restorative healing also takes time. It doesn't necessarily mean that things will go back to normal, but it can mean that the new normal is even better than before. In some instances, we may not see the lasting effects of restoration this side of heaven.

Hannah did the work of restoration in her own heart toward her birth mom, Cindy. Hannah left a note for Cindy extending her forgiveness, a forgiveness Cindy didn't ask for. At the conclusion of the movie we see Cindy's redemption, but Hannah does not. The viewer is left to wonder if that relationship ever went beyond the handwritten note. In the end, it doesn't matter. Forgiveness was extended and 19 years worth of restoration was born in Cindy's heart.

> In what way do you need to do the hard work of restoration
> in your relationships?

It is not outside the realm of possibility that there is a current relationship or an old, forgotten one that needs some attention.

YOUR CHALLENGE NEXT WEEK

As you conclude this final week of study, indicate which of the four weeks was most eye-opening for you, in the space that follows.

Each of these topics could generate an entire study all its own. In fact, each of them has resulted in numerous studies. (We've listed a few at the end of this page; also see *www.lifeway.com* and p. 61.) Perhaps your participation in this small group has revealed in you a desire to continue a path of study down one particular road introduced in this experience. Perhaps issues surrounding your secret sins and struggles with identity have surfaced after years of suppression, and now you have to engage the hard work of confession, forgiveness, and restoration. Continue to trust our God who has led you this far; He will continue to do so!

Take this final opportunity to journal in response to the questions on pages 54–55. Be challenged to open up and share this part of your story with someone this week. It can be your spouse, another family member, or close friend. Ask whether he or she would allow you to share what you have learned, including as much of your story as you feel free to share.

Surrendering the Secret: Healing the Heartbreak of Abortion, by Pat Layton
Breaking Free: Making Liberty in Christ a Reality in Life, by Beth Moore
Selected studies in the Picking up the Pieces series (such as addictions, depression, and helps on providing a healing ministry to others)

Answer both of the following questions.

1   What were the most valuable insights you gleaned from the *OCTOBER BABY* movie?

2 Where have the discoveries during this study led you in your relationship with Jesus Christ?

End Notes

A Note to Leaders

1. David Platt, "Secret Church: Marriage, Family, Sex, and the Gospel" (LifeWay simulcast event, The Church at Brook Hills, Birmingham, AL, November 4, 2011).

Session 1

1. Jeannie St. John Taylor, *You Wouldn't Love Me If You Knew* (Nashville, TN: Abingdon Press, 2003).
2. David M. Fleming and Russell Fuller, "Book of Psalms," *Holman Illustrated Bible Dictionary* (Nashville, TN: Holman Bible Publishers, 2003), 1342–44.
3. Spiros Zodhiates, ed., *Hebrew-Greek Key Word Study Bible* (Chattanooga, TN: AMP Publishers, 2008), 3064.
4. William Shakespeare, *Macbeth,* ed. Kenneth Muir, Arden Shakespeare (London: Methuen Drama, 1984), 44. Available from the Internet: *www.amazon.com*

Session 2

1. "The Search for Identity-The Teenage Struggle," Family University [online, cited 10 January 2012]. Available from the Internet: *www.family-university.org/archive/search_identity.html*
2. Stewart D. Friedman and Jeffrey H. Greenhaus, *Work and Family-Allies or Enemies?* (New York: Oxford University Press, 2000), 230. Available from the Internet *http://books. google.com*
3. Ibid.
4. *The American Heritage® Dictionary of the English Language,* 4th ed. (Boston: Houghton Mifflin Company, 2000), [online, cited 10 January 2012]. Available from the Internet: *www.thefreedictionary.com/identity+crisis*
5. *HCSB Study Bible* (Nashville, TN: Holman Bible Publishers, 2010), 1237.
6. Adapted from "God Treasures Us!" Persevering Counseling Ministries [online, cited 10 January 2012]. Available from the Internet: *www.persevering.org/perceiv.html*

Session 3

1. Alexander Pope, "An Essay on Criticism," The EServer Poetry Collection [online, cited 10 January 2012]. Available from the Internet: *http://poetry.eserver.org/essay-on-criticism.html*

Session 4

1. Walter A. Elwell, "Reconciliation," *Baker's Evangelical Dictionary of Theology* [online, cited 10 January 2012]. Available from the Internet: *www.biblestudytools.com/ dictionaries/bakers-evangelical-dictionary*
2. Walter A. Elwell, "Restore, Renew," *Baker's Evangelical Dictionary of Theology* [online, cited 10 January 2012]. Available from the Internet: *www.biblestudytools.com/ dictionaries/bakers-evangelical-dictionary*
3. John MacArthur, *The MacArthur Bible Commentary* (Nashville, TN: Thomas Nelson, 2005), 1426.
4. Ibid.
5. Ibid., 1426–27.

JESUS

Jesus Christ was with God the Father before the world was created. He became human and lived among humanity as Jesus of Nazareth. He came to show us what God the Father is like. He lived a sinless life, showing us how to live; and He died on a cross to pay for our sins. God raised Him from the dead.

Jesus is the source of eternal life. Jesus wants to be the doorway to new life for you. In the Bible He was called the "Lamb of God" (John 1:29). In the Old Testament, sacrifices were made for the sins of the people. Jesus became the sacrificial Lamb offered for your sin.

Jesus said, "I am the way, the truth, and the life. No one comes to the Father except through Me" (John 14:6). He is waiting for you now.

> Admit to God that you are a sinner. Repent, turning away from your sin.

> By faith receive Jesus Christ as God's Son and accept Jesus' gift of forgiveness from sin. He took the penalty for your sin by dying on the cross.

> Confess your faith in Jesus Christ as Savior and Lord.

You may pray a prayer similar to this as you call on God to save you: "Dear God, I know that You love me. I confess my sin and my need of salvation. I turn away from my sin and place my faith in Jesus as my Savior and Lord. In Jesus' name I pray, amen."

After you have received Jesus Christ into your life, tell a pastor or another Christian friend about your decision. Show others your faith in Christ by asking for baptism by immersion in your local church as a public expression of your faith.

Leader Notes

Prepare for an exciting adventure as you facilitate an *Every Life Is Beautiful* small group. The combination of the movie with the study can lead many participants to start or continue the healing process. Some significant issues may surface as they learn to tell parts of their stories to close, trusted people—and to realize that God can use for good even a shameful part of their past. A group can be a significant means of personal support.

This four-week study may be the impetus some women need to engage in other Bible studies, such as *Surrendering the Secret*, or in ongoing affinity groups. For example, adoptive moms might decide to get together in homes once a month to talk about issues they and their children face.

Look over information about this study and watch the movie again if possible. (This study assumes participants have seen *OCTOBER BABY*.) Especially note the small-group guidelines on page 11. Just as you will be asking your group to commit to those guidelines, affirm them yourself. Pray about the individuals who potentially will attend: for their needs, their families, their past and present, and the privilege to participate with them.

This study is ideal for women, especially young women or any small group of adults. Some will have a personal interest, such as adoption, or an issue in their past, such as abortion, and may be interested but hesitant. As you promote the study, don't neglect people who simply loved *OCTOBER BABY!* This is a nice study to conduct in homes and is good outreach for your church.

Your resources include *Every Life Is Beautiful: The OCTOBER BABY Bible Study* member and *Every Life Is Beautiful: The OCTOBER BABY Bible Study* DVD leader kit (item 005508071). Movie clips and a movie trailer are on the Bible study DVD.

Read through the entire member book and then go back and prepare for each session with your group in mind. Make notes and go deep into the

Scriptures. Consider ways to involve learners. Most groups can meet for an hour, but you can expand the schedule if time and location allow. Be sure to include prayer. These are the suggested time frames.

15 minutes	**Opening and Share**
10 minutes	**Watch and discuss**
20 minutes	**Study and discuss**
15 minutes	**Live and closure**

After the first session, let group members briefly share insights from their between-week Challenges. Include as part of your opening Share time.

While sensitive, deep issues may surface, know that the overall themes of *Every Life Is Beautiful* are ones with which all people grapple. Learners are given options about which questions to answer, and no one should be forced to share. Be sensitive to group dynamics and willing to spend extra time with anyone who may need it. Recognize your limits, though; don't hesitate to offer a referral especially if you sense danger. Have trusted people you can call on in your church or community.

A student edition (member book, item 005888879 and kit, item 005512172) is also available. Themes are the same as this study, with appropriate applications for teens and collegians. Three clips are also the same.

Clip descriptions and lengths:

Clip 1: The Secret Revealed (4:16)
Hannah finds her birth mother.

Clip 2: "I Don't Even Know Me" (4:34)
Hannah chooses a favorite place to deal with the emotions and questions about her personal identity.

Clip 3: You Have the Power to Forgive (6:51)
In the beauty of a cathedral, Hannah discovers the forgiveness she needs—and the power to give it.

Clip 4: "Thank You for Wanting Me" (3:08)
God's restoration is evident in many lives.

Visit *www.lifeway.com/octoberbaby* for downloads of these clips.

Eight Steps to Healing

From Surrendering the Secret: Healing the Heartbreak of Abortion
by Pat Layton

1. **Share the story**—Sharing is the first step toward recovery, freedom, and healing.
2. **Look at the truth about abortion**—During this healing step a woman is exposed to the truth about abortion as a profitable industry, the truth about the unborn child, abortion procedures, and what God's Word teaches about abortion.
3. **Recognize the healthy side of anger**—Acknowledging and releasing anger in healthy ways are important to complete healing. God uses this stage to clarify responsibility and ultimate repentance.
4. **Take the next step: pursue forgiveness**—After understanding and embracing anger, God wants post-abortive men and women to forgive and receive forgiveness. Experiencing forgiveness creates deep peace and joy in the lives of those once held captive.
5. **Recognize the differences between grief and guilt and work through each**—A healthy grief process and a safe place enables a woman to deal with the grief and guilt that follow an abortion decision—and a loss most of the world has no idea how to embrace.
6. **Allow God to exchange bondage for freedom**—Isaiah 61 provides a wonderful backdrop for God to exchange past secrets, shame, false beliefs, and distorted perspectives for His immeasurable grace and restoration.
7. **Conduct a release/memorial service**—A gentle memorial service allows post-abortive men and women to mourn the loss of their unborn child, to comfort one another, and to be comforted by others who have experienced the pain of a past abortion.
8. **Share healing through the word of your testimony**—God wants to use our stories and the truth we now understand to help other women and men who struggle with past decisions (see Rev. 12:11).

Follow-up Resources
Grief and Suffering
Holding on to Hope: A Pathway Through Suffering to the Heart of God
  by Nancy Guthrie
I Will Carry You: The Sacred Dance of Grief and Joy by Angie Smith
Empty Arms: Coping After Miscarriage, Stillbirth and Infant Death
  by Sherokee Isle
A Guide for Fathers: When a Baby Dies by Tim Nelson
Forgotten Tears, A Grandmother's Journey Through Grief
  by Nina Bennett
I'll Hold You in Heaven by Jack Hayford
Perinatal Comfort Care, Tampa *(ComfortCare.com)*; Carolina Perinatal
  Support Network, North Carolina *(PerinatalComfortCare.org)*

For Adoptive Parents
The Connected Child: Bring Hope and Healing to Your Adoptive Family
  by Karyn Purvis (nation's leading expert and a Christian)
Successful Adoption: A Guide for Christian Families
  by Natalie Nichols Gillespie
"My Baby and Me" series by Anne Pierson (*www.lovingandcaring.org*):
  Basic Decision Making; Looking at Adoption; A Place to Call Home
So I Was Thinking About Adoption: Considering Your Choices
  by Mardie Caldwell
*Adopted for Life: The Priority of Adoption for Christian Families
  and Churches* by Russell Moore
Twenty Things Adopted Kids Wish Their Adoptive Parents Knew
  by Sherrie Eldridge

For Adopted Children
Did My First Mother Love Me? by Kathryn Ann Miller
Adoption Is for Always by Linda Walvoord Girard
My Adopted Child, There's No One Like You by Dr. Kevin Leman

Infertility
The Ache for a Child by Debra Birdwell
Empty Womb, Aching Heart by Marlo Schalesky

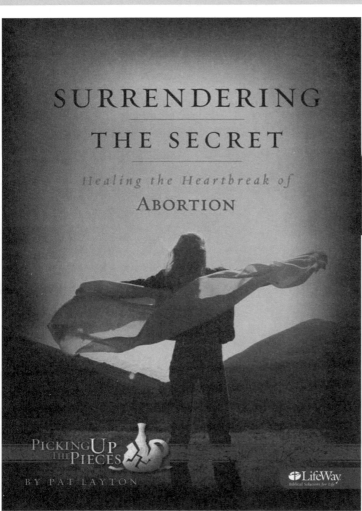
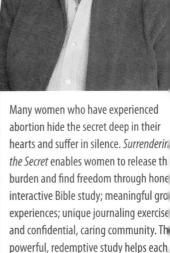